Daniel Tyler-Ray

The Slow Glow of Winter

Omecronom

For more information, please visit www.tyler-ray.net

© 2013 Omecronon

ISBN no: 978-91-87713-99-6

Table of Contents

1. Attempt
2. The Glow After Afterglow
3. We All Have Our Fancies ...
4. McGuinn Was Right (I Take It)
5. Unvacuumised
6. The Restaurant
7. Yesterday I Wrote this Song
8. Conditions of Me
9. A Million Shortcomings
10. Scattered in the Absent Wind
11. Abhorrent Thoughts
12. Philosophical Crime Affair
13. Size Does Matter
14. The Slow Glow of Winter Gone
15. A Life in a World
16. Notes from Above Ground
17. Black Web
18. Shade of Moon
19. Finale

The Slow Glow of Winter

Attempt

I will truly ask

If it's in me to do it?

Painting the sublime ...

The Glow After Afterglow

Yesterday's saturation is all a memory now,
And the promise of this shining day seems
To have left me jaded for a moment
Before I took my eyes where I put them,
In compelling grass,
Outside the shallow cave
The other day it seems.

Lapis Lazuli shimmering ...
A soft whirlwind;
Oh how crowns of trees play
Muddle, muddle
With my senses
As dusk awaits.

It's on the wind for certain.
A dim moon is anticipated
Only to conjure up a night;
A diminished satellite forgotten,
While it brings sleep.

(The nimbus of a gate)

Wide asleep in unknown havens,

A Morian box awaits...

Will the key suffice or suffer

From this dreamscape?

An ocean to part company with,

Where seagulls never sleep;

Prometheus and an eagle.

(An interim of chaotic motion of fern)

The Greek cradle I was born in is set ashore;

And Spartan waves of incense

Did speak to me of innocence

Once upon a brittle time;

Why not speak of feathers yet to be?

A bonfire gone in multiverse,

The multiversa open;

Prodigies in becoming?

Then the chant of Coptic lands,

Where pyramids dwell in Mathematical precision.

Waters unfolded and the priestess is lost

In the riddle of her own mind…

A Moiran box awaits; behold the mysteries,

Of ancient worlds and beautiful spaces,

Butterflies in metaphor air…

I would fly with them still.

Night is a wildfire; glowing eyes

Seek a raven's treasure, not a faraway beach,

And the Bosporus opens the gates of the horizon

That can only be traversed in dream or transmigration.

It speaks in a Sufis' circle;

The long forgotten Persia

We call yesterday…

Hagia Sophia speaks to me;

As if I could sacrifice

Being a mere one

Among the myriad creatures;

Lao speaks in the soft cloth

Of yesterday's anticipation

And Amritsar shines from a distance

In high air

Where the refreshed eye of my imagination

Sometimes will be...

Let east and west intertwine;

Fertilize futures yet to be seen...

Let us not believe in mere angels

And devils...

Bring on the lights,

Of ancient tales

That whisper sweet music

In our forgotten ears...

The blue mosque;

Constant in Opal hindsight,

To make the future shine!

There is no more sound;

Only moist voices

From the humid haven

Of my feather-like mind;

A siren wind passes gently,

And so I hesitate once more

At the gate of it all;

Just like it was the end of the line ...

We All Have our Fancies …

To add it up: it was a rather sunny day in late August 2013. I was terribly disappointed because my dog had left me for another. I didn't fulfil her needs, the dog told me. I inhaled the brisk wind sighing. Who fulfilled her needs then? Another dog? She didn't tell me; she just left.

I have a history with dogs. I like their company even though I can't remember a single one that I've been with at the moment. We all have our peculiarities, now don't we? There's nothing wrong with being hung up on dogs, now is there? I mean face it! We all need someone to love and if a dog is man's best friend then it seems pretty normal to get engaged. I think Voltaire might have agreed with me or at least he would have died for my right to have that opinion. I must be the most enlightened guy in the neighborhood. Everyone else has been pretty nasty because I was with a dog.

There was this woman a while back. She told me she was falling in love. On rare occasions women actually say things like that; they don't just, as would be rather normal, wait for the guy to make the first move. But I told her to forget me. Why, she asked. I told her that I fancied dogs and that I had one; a stable relationship. She immediately told me that she was falling out of love then. I wonder to myself even this day if she was completely normal.

McGuinn was Right (I Take It)

I never was in Rio;

Never did return...

The space between

The you and the me

Has slowly grown

Small fingers,

And

From a remote living room

There is a solemn shriek;

Parallel worlds

Converge

Of sadness

'Cause winter's bliss

Is yet to come of age;

In a dry and maddened space

We live and lift a finger;

Pull a lie,

To a lever,

Here we live,

And there's no trace,

Of humility in the estranged Metro

Once called free...

Is there anyone in space?

Unvacuumised

I can't remember the name of the game;
I just remember to wear and to bear
My shame,
In someone else's name.

To see apart from a point of view,
Try develop a photograph
Of dew,
For someone old and new.

Holy waters, stones unturned,
Ancient quarters, bones unburned.

I just came in by the door one day,
Leaving all of your guild astray
In vain;
Alas I hide in an ocean of pain.

The antidote's like a wasted wine;
Tries its best not to intertwine

In fear,

A hologram in a world I smear.

The Reastaurant

I picked the most prestigeous

And expensive restaurant in town

Only to have a splendid dinner

And then escape from the place

I went there and the waitor

Showed me a table, handing me

The exclusive menu.

Going through the menu I

Finally picked a very expensive meal

And to that I added

A sublime South African wine

Having finished the dinner I waited for a short while

Nobody gave me any attention

Judging the timing to be correct I rose

From the table and headed for the door

Having noticed the waitor wasn't too far away

I was lucky!

The waiter came up to me and said

"What are you doing sir?"

"Getting out of here."

"You can't do that, sir."

"So. What are you going to do about it, then?"

"I feel somewhat embarrassed to say it sir but you have a stain on your jacket."

Hmm. That was a rather strange way of approaching a criminal.

"A stain on my jacket? So what?"

"Well sir. You can't leave the restaurant in such a poor condition. Leave the jacket with us. We'll get it cleaned for you."

"That would be very kind of you but aren't you going to call the police?"

"What for?"

"Well. I've had dinner here for an average year's salary and I won't pay for it."

"The stain is more important. It would harm our image if you left us in that condition."

"Your image?"

"Yes."

"But what about the bill?"

"The federal bank reserve owns this restaurant, it's good for their book-keeping."

"But surely you must do something!"

"Oh well. The bill is only 50 cent so it's on the house."

"50 cent? Why's that?"

"We suggest that it's very questionable if 1+1=2. Since we're owned by the federal bank reserve we have the right to treat Mathematics adequately, and so your bill adds up to 50 cents, sir."

"But won't that harm the restaurant pretty much? You might go bankrupt."

"Well. The IRS is into religion, believing in numbers and so. We're more into science here."

I can't go to jail. And apparently I wouldn't qualify for a job as a waiter. Just my luck.

"Would you care for some more wine sir? It costs 1000 dollars but it's on the house."

Yesterday I Wrote this Song

Today is the day; the very peak of my life thus far. You see; yesterday I wrote this song and I feel very confident about it. It's only a matter of getting the right singer for it and then I can quit my job as an insurance salesman for good; the song is destined to succeed.

Everything about it smells like success. The very opening will take the listener by storm; a whirlwind to be more precise. The opening words are:

And now, the end is near
And so I face the final curtain

That's not too bad, is it? No, I tell you straight from my bubbely, bubbely heart that it will be a huge hit; something for many generations to remember and relate to and it was me and nobody else who wrote it. Earlier today I chatted with someone on the phone and she said it was taken. I was taken by complete surprise. Is there a copycat already? I mean – I only just wrote it! It was yesterday. I told the lady on the phone that I was going to call the song "My Way" and she responded her way so I suppose that she can relate to it too if she could only get it out of her head that it's taken.

My friend, I say it clear
I state my case, of which I'm certain

Yes! Those lines will really stick with the listener. Maybe lady Gaga is interested. She could do it playing the piano. I hope she has the voice for it. If anyone has done it her way it's she. It will fit her image so well. I'll do some research in finding her agent and then I'll give them an offer they simply can't refuse.

Conditions of Me*

Well I'm here trying to pretend I'm a man

Just waiting for the perfect screw

I look for the drill and find it lost in a pile

Another nasty concept of you

A thin nail with a point of view

At times I feel like turning lest betray my wife

'cause Kari-Ann is one of my toys

My lover couldn't do it so I have my life

I can't even comply to the boys, oh no

For boys will be boys will be boys

They say love's a gamble hard to win easy lose

And when sun shines all always say nay

I guess life is a fable and faith doesn't heal

Then when the chics call where they may

Then Kari-Ann is here to stay

And as I was shifting drill to go my way

I could not shake away the nail – nooo

I took out Mailer when I felt the gloom

I'll never see my wife again oh no

She told me Kari-Ann was gay – that way

So tell me, teach me, what can I do

Who knows where I'm going to stay?

I've learned from my mistakes but I can't take advice

And play pool is not at all cool

Snooker's the thing around noon

Old folks may know what to do

Kari-Ann is whistling the tune

I won't drill unless I'm with you

*May not be well received in Britain …

A Million Shortcomings

There was a day, not too long ago, when all my shortcomings failed; I became successful. My, oh my! What does that mean? Do I have to change my wardrobe, my lifestyle, my friends even? Are my friends not good enough for me anymore?

Moving in circles as it were, trying to find a way to breathe the subtle and deceitful air of success I finally came up with a solution. A change of wardrobe wasn't really necessary since I always had seemed to overdo it; it was perfect for a successful person. Changing friends on the other hand took me quite a while to figure out. My friends had always meant the world to me and in this new atmosphere of blinding success the light, blinding indeed, didn't seem to make room for more than contacts. Can contacts be friends I wondered to myself? Yes, maybe… and yet maybe not. That's for time to tell I reckon. As far as time's concerned it's elusive indeed in this strange air of success.

It's funny how all you ever dreamt of comes to you like a plague; I could never compete with Marilyn nor Bruce Lee nor anyone else for that matter and the line between being successful and infamous seemed to be quite blurry; I might prefer the latter to the former in a way. There's a million reasons why; all my shortcomings to put it plain. I am indeed aware of them and maybe one day, if the bastard press allows, I might be able to put them on display for the world to see. I will then be infamous, a dwarf instead of a lion, and my days in the deceptive air of success will be numbered. My house will be haunted and I will be all gone; pretty gone.

Then, when the day comes and I am infamous I will tell my story to an adjacent moon shining in defiant fervor and it will surely laugh at me, like they're all laughing at me (on a temporary basis; tomorrow the headlines will focus on something else).

Scattered in the Absent Wind

Estranged by adorers,
Scattered in the absent wind;
This vacuum is a bird of prey.
Too late for the news of the world;
Too soon for the fascination
Strangers bring to light.

"Could there be tomorrow",
I asked a hollow mirror,
Begging the question
To respond;
Late night in Jericho Street,
We howl our goodbyes.

Abhorrent Thoughts

I have no apple tree

To entice Newton

To stick around;

I only have a stick to burn,

Abhorrent thoughts

Of stormy weather,

Are all you youngsters

So damn clever,

As to forget the springs

To come of age;

The evenings speak

Of summer rage,

And gladness like

Spilled milk

To the lions.

Oh August sun!

I will remember you,

In future tense.

Philosophical Crime Affair

Plastic highway ...
A man reaches out
for a gun,
but unfortunately
for him
It's been put there
by Schopenhauer...

In distresse
Crawling vampires
in a film
starring Paul Ree
take me over
and I try to do the same
failing
as would be natural.

In desperation
I buy a plastic gun,
Looking very real

And go to the nearest bank.

At the counter I say:

"Give me all your money or

I'll shoot all of you!"

The lady on the other side of the counter responds:

"That piece seems slightly gunnish to me"

"What do you mean? It's a gun and I'm serious.

Hand me the money!"

"Well sir. It may be a gun or a non-gun

but it may also be gunnish"

"What the hell do you mean? A gun is a gun and a non-gun is a non-gun. This is a gun so hand me the money!"

"Only because that thing seems gunnish it doesn't entail that it is neither a gun nor a non-gun sir."

"Forget about the bloody gun then. Just hand me the money! All of it."

"Sorry sir, but I can't do that."

"Why?"

"It's not in line with our bank policy to

 hand money over to robbers unless they express

 themselves in synthetic a priori expressions sir."

"I don't care about your bank policy! Just give me the money."

"I would break the law by doing so. I simply can't.
 Otherwise I'd be happy to assist you sir."
"But since I haven't expressed myself properly,
 Won't you call the police?"
"No sir. It's a bank policy but it's not a federal crime."

Leaving the bank weeping I went straight to Kaliningrad.

Size Does Matter

We met in a bar. It was a pale evening slowly approaching midnight even thought not too late and we both had a drink; it was cool and dry, the atmosphere could have been smoky some fifty years ago and the piano player near the corner of the room was playing a simple tune; to play simple is an art indeed. The bar wasn't too crowded and it wasn't very noisy. The lady was cool, sophisticated and we had a good time talking; interesting things about matters not everyone knows about or talks about much; she was special. Her ways enticed me to go further and so I did, although being hesitant at first. She had a faint aura of elegance and grace; she was all that!

Minutes turned to quarters and I sat there feeling spellbound by her while at the same time making my plans for the right way; the right move. I was hoping that it didn't show but something about her told me that she was thinking along the same lines. I was content with that and let the feeling go.

The conversation went on nicely; we had a very good time. I could tell that she, at times, talked in ways that tended to be a little standard, like she was in the mood; I wouldn't know. Wishful thinking? I didn't think so. So I hooked on to those lines of hers when they appeared. It seemed to work alright. I guess it was just that – alright!

After quite some time she asked me in a low and slow voice, only slightly hinting at romance, if we could leave. I said yes. Having risen from the bar I suddenly realized what hadn't been visible to me before. The lady was a dwarf. So much for sophistication I suppose. I made a weird excuse and left the bar terribly disappointed.

The Slow Glow of Winter Gone

I used to be almost frantically in love with her; everything about her in fact. If it wasn't her turtle neck smile then it was the things she said every morning when we woke up; soothing words and always something slightly witty. What a way to start a day!

Melting snow surrounded the little house, placed miles from nowhere it seemed even though it didn't lack neighbors. Solitude paints a grim mask on anyone it seems and I miss her to this day.

I had to get out and help the snow disappear; the little snow there was, that is. A spade is a spade alright and so I grabbed mine and got to work which was pretty easy; it was rather warm and yesterday's flakes had only touched the ground gently although nighttime made it a little harder.

The house wasn't derelict really; it was only in need of some insulation. I enjoyed the evenings by the modest fireplace as much as I could; very handy this time of year. The fire mirrored in the windows so much that it was in fact quite a sight looking out. Woodland not too far away and a small hill too. One could be worse off than miles from nowhere, but where are the guests that used to come here? When we parted, sadly, most of our mutual friends parted too. It seemed like just being one wasn't good enough and yet I can still remember all the good times, refusing to succumb to merely being mellow or nostalgic. One makes up one's history and I've chosen - no - I've tried hard to neglect the painful times, the times we were arguing, opposing one another like strangers. Of course we knew each others' faults; we'd been around for quite some time. However, there are things a person can never escape from, or so it seems to me. Refusing to think of it as anything else than a benefit, an experience, won't do since it's so scary for so many who simply don't know what it is.

Oh, how time passes slowly in this little den of mine where I hide not being able to hold back a tear thinking. I think too much perhaps.

Winter's all dead and gone as I drink forgetfulness out of an empty, broken cup that I tried to make shine. A new season awaits and with it comes the shine for sure. Yesterday's seaweed smells awkward and bears memories of lost conquests under a sky turned crimson; so subtly the clouds seem to move above my head. A quiet breeze and all of a sudden it's not Zen or is it? She stands there in front of me; her name is unknown to me as it would be for others (strangers, passing by).

I miss her still, yet I can't blame her for leaving me. I'm impossible really. I want to have children but I can never, ever have any and she knew; she knows.

I don't have any family. Or should I say I don't have any contact with my family. My parents won't speak to me; out of shame perhaps.

Maybe you know my little secret. I once was diagnosed. I took pills, drugs, for years and then one day, when the time was ripe, I let the pills go. Eventually I was cured and stable but no doctor wanted to believe in it. They all wanted me ill, sick, and stuffed with the drugs. I was in and out of hospitals. I faked taking the pills in order not to disturb my neurochemical balance. People even tried their best to make a fool out of me since I was considered a threat to them. And so there were all kinds of rumours around. I remain sane to this day but I can never, ever, have a child.

Just think of it! If I had, let's say, a daughter. Sooner or later, by the age of 6 perhaps, my daughter would come home to me sobbing and say "Father! They tell me you are... Am I that too?" I suppose that the picture is clearly visible. I can't be responsible for hurting my child that way. Just consider for a moment the pressure on a fragile child's mind; the fear and the weariness. "Am I like my father? Is it in me too?" Questions like that, uncertainties, can linger for many, many painful years. In my imagination I can hear my baby daughter crying herself to sleep all alone and there's little I can do really. I mean – I'm the monster in her or am I not?

How I miss her! She left me and they will all leave me; always. I wish that damn etiquette would vanish! Diagnoses are so overused and overstated. That's the terrible thing about it. It doesn't mean a damn thing, it's just an instrument of power for the doctors who are above the legal system always. Their word is almost never questioned. However, there are things that enlighten those who search; peripherical researchers and doctors who are peripheral for a reason; they know there are cures because they've done the experiments and found out. However there's money involved; money and the mob. Little has changed for 2000 years it sometimes seems.

The slow glow of winter is gone. I light a modest candle in my little den to remind myself of her. No nostalgia for me. Simply allow me to rest here in the memory of her for a short while and what we could have become if not for me. If the light is blue it's only momentous blue.

A Life in a World

Gem haunt;
Exaggerated dreamchase ...
The humid haven
That is our interior landscape,
Made up by some Lebenswelt
Or so,

(I shouldn't come on pretentious)

Tells us to go on
In the madness which is
Everyday existence;

(Existence is a word that means nothing)

Like fragile children
We are crushed;
Our heads to the ground
With hearts like elephants
We can love despite all this.

Love may not be the solution,

But is man and womans'

Private and secret dream

By which they strive

With minds intact.

(On rainy islands they don't like umbrellas much; it's art)

Nightmare descends into Jericho city,

And the fields are as wasteland;

Like in the poem.

(Oh China, China! How you suffer!)

The drunken moon looks down,

And smiles as of arrogance

While chaos reigns,

Made up by the desolate spirits

That still haunts our feeble minds ...

Will we ever escape this curse?

Notes from Above Ground

Before I live I write this message. There might be secrets for you to know as my feet were below the ground that fed me like a solemn plant that whispered secrets in my mute ear; I didn't hear. Duty? Oh yeah! A crime was committed and it was the headlines; the bastard press as usual. Synergy! Oh how it's created. We manufacture disasters every day. I bet the opium is running as low as alcohol; not at all. Will east and west ever meet I wonder? I put a spell on me because I'm mine and I'm not free but born to stay; to stick around. The coffin was simply too small and I had to rise and at the same time make myself smaller. Quite an enterprise! Never was there any mountain to climb. Mountains are for adorers; we could be them if we want to.

The words came to a brisk halt. Chaos but also a promise for a new beginning. The big bully is not as big as it used to be perhaps and Latin winds will hopefully spread across the land that has a patent in its name for an entire continent. L'America is L'America, America and L'Amérique for sure; let's face that fact and by all means try to stay together.

They say Canadian mosquitos make a somewhat different sound than the Nordic and the Russian ones. I wouldn't know. The Russian and Nordic ones are probably keen on Vodka whereas the Canadian ones tend to fancy wine I reckon. I like wine. Never was a Vodka drinker; no offence to anyone. My taste is my taste and I don't intend to impose it on others. Canada might suit me though.

Sting ray! What a name. Vehicles come and go and Tibet is open for that reason. Yes indeed. That's Ford for yah. Never mind the brands; let's settle for vehicles even though "car" more often than not is the first word a young child learns. "Vehicle" is a wider category; save that for later. I'll live 'til the day a 3-year old says "Daddy! Audi!"

So! What to do here above ground? From the point of view of integrity I might have managed to as good as I can. This cannot be $\sum x+\infty$ because we're finite. It's just that I just rose and the rose spells Amanda. I wish I could reach her; she's had a rough time. Hey you! It's not over yet. The clock is still ticking normally, it's just a bully that's been torn as it lives in a bubble. The gates of the horizon are questioned; bolts unlocked and we live in a fragile society. I hope things will be better after I've had a small dish; at least my mind will be elsewhere. I wouldn't know what to call it but it somehow rhymes with an Austrian phenomenon. Much needed. What's wrong anyway but a lot. Now everything here is flooded.

I have my space – my space in which to breathe and I'm thankful for that. We are not free. Freedom is a buzzword; nothing else. There are so many buzzwords. Bastard press! Bastard universe. The multiversa makes up parallel spaces for us to have a glance at. I was always younger than yesterday; I must have forgotten that while in the coffin. Misery? Oh yeah! I'm grateful for the misery because it helped me grow. Misery can help people grow if you believe it will.

Let's not believe in angels and devils in this world. Nothing is black and white and I disagree with one American writer; John Steinbeck. People are not born evil. People are shaped and they also shape themselves. Look who's talking! Did I shape the coffin? No sir! The coffin needed another craft than mine to be built.

Another American informed me that Nihilism meant that nothing matters. It doesn't! Nihilism simply states that there are no values in morals. That is to say that there are no values unless we create them; that's what we need to do. People can hate religion but what they really hate, I reckon, is the political use of it. People often need guiding principles. Personally I'm stuffed with them, perhaps to stuffed, I was almost mummified; I'd like to give that to you my reader.

We need to take care of each other otherwise we're wasted. I hope the big bully has learned that. Truths can be hard at times; any Indian knows that. It's hard to invert a dream; it doesn't work out easily.

I'm looking for a woman simply because I like their company. We have a lot in common. I wish for my friend; I hope for them and if it would do any good I could get down on my knees and pray for them all. I never left them! I admit having been angry in disenchanted times but a man is only a man; what can he do? I'm not looking for a car. Some things never come back even though we can think of it that way even though Robert Kennedy probably was quite a guy. So was Martin Luther King I reckon. Elvis was just a man...if "just" is the word for it. Oh how fame rapes! People can be nostalgic. I don't intend to conjure up anything like that since it's not me. My naïveté is too strong at times I'm afraid. All angels of hell can go home – the wars could be over. We have other things to think about these days and that's to mend what's broken by the 20:th century. The new millennium certainly didn't start well – it's been a slippery slope. Bastard universe! I hope and if I can I pray that we've reached a turning point. Even Los Angeles and London suffer now and then.

I have a dream! I want to go to Israel and from there to Iran to see Pakistan and reach India. Amritsar! Never been there but lions don't corrode. I'm in love with Sufism but I don't know if that's understood nor well seen. There are a lot of them. I've been an Indian hiding in the feathered clouds but now I'm back from the coffin where it sent me... By Indian I perhaps mean that I have dreams. I CAN be a visionary but it sent me to the coffin. I don't know why I have to pay for my life. My friends! I hope that you're with me still, even from a distance. I don't aim to touch from a distance; that would be crude since the expression is taken.

So take care ladies and gentemen. Bueno! Let's stop there now; there's a hippo living in all of us; it's easy to forget that. I think they're cute myself. Entschuldigung aber Ich kann nicht Deutch sprechen - you might notice that from the spelling. Dresden is not feeling good at the moment. Been there a while back. It was all like a huge grass field. I remember a church without a roof. Guilt by accusation. I now recall my favourite Tarkovskij movie. It's all in black and white except the end when it turns to colours. 4 hours of pure magic!

I'd better stick to something more familiar. We need to stay together, now won't we; or else what have we learned so far?

Let me be
Fractalabstractimmediate;
The language wind
That carries
My name…

Let me develop
Pictures of earth!

Let me experience chaos
In the motion
Of fern.

Let me be microscope wind
Touching your face.

A facial structure can be beautiful, regardless of age. It's how we're moulded and how we mould ourselves that matters. Please tame the beast that is within me and turn it into a hippo…not a hype.

Enamoured with a jaded moon by my side; I do not strive for comfort in the ugly city where all I hear are the explosions of the future. If I can break a brick I would before the light flickers and spirits rise to the sky as to greet the bagpipe moon as seen from within.

Black Web

Through unknowns waters

Phenomena slide

My gaze in hazy

Pearl strewn pathways

Coming on …

Come with me!

Let us transcend

Into the mystic

Silk layered

Cat-like tokens

Where dawn sighs

At last.

Tant y soit possible

Et je reste ici

Avec les temps

Dans mon âme …

L'Amazon

Où je te perde

Et te rétrouve

Pour des instants

L'un après l'autre ...

Le pont en tremblant

Cessasion;

Je suis le tien.

Shade of Moon

The shade of moon

Tells tales of the now.

Now can the silent wind

Of yesterday's toil

Rest in my refreshed mind.

Too blind from yesterdays

To see, clearly,

The tomorrows to come;

A feudal season,

A blurry sky ...

(Laughing in absence it seems)

The shade of moon

Tells tales I might not want to hear,

And yet I listen

For the sake of its beauty

Finale

There once was a mermaid too hard to apprehend. We could hear her breathing as the earthquake fell down upon us; we're simply being superstitious and that's the problem. No need really as daily life progresses and we must get by; get along. So I say, let's sing this 21:th century song for the young to come for we borrowed the land and we, the most spoiled generation there is, would be the one who is acting like a collective vampire whose prey it seems, is tomorrow.

No doubt in my mind that we are guilty. Numerology was never the thing; it was something invented.

(Not in nature but imposed on it).

Hence the dead didn't rise on the day of the dead, and many years will go by when little occurs but the stupidity of man, the ugly face of man, for man doesn't think more than one step at a time. I, myself, have a great deal to learn… not unlike my ancestors and the generations to come. They ripe what we sow; we – the spoiled ones who just happened to live in a certain time, taking advantage of it, exhausting resources. No wonder there will be no trace of us some 5000 years from now unless something miraculous happens. What will it be I wonder? When can we learn to lift others up instead of living at the expense of others?

The shade of moon
Tells tales I might not want to hear,
And yet I listen
For the sake of its beauty.

Yet I listen for the sake of its beauty.

The Slow Glow of Winter

The Slow Glow of Winter